LIVING
HOPE
FOR THE
HEART

LIVING
HOPE
FOR THE
HEART

A Collection of God-Centered, Biblically Inspired Poetry

by Elicia Roy

Living Hope For the Heart – A Collection of God-Centered, Biblically Inspired Poetry

www.livinghopefortheheart.org

© 2019 by Elicia Roy

Printed in the United States of America

Published by Living Hope For The Heart

Scriptures taken from the Holy Bible, New International Version®, NIV®. Copyright © 1973, 1978, 1984, 2011 by Biblica, Inc.™ Used by permission of Zondervan. All rights reserved worldwide. www.zondervan.com The "NIV" and "New International Version" are trademarks registered in the United States Patent and Trademark Office by Biblica, Inc.™

Library of Congress Cataloging – in Publication Data

Roy, Elicia.

Living Hope For the Heart – A Collection of God-Centered, Biblically Inspired Poetry

ISBN 9781072712640

1. Christian poetry 2. Devotional – Christianity 3. Inspirational writing

Acknowledgements

This work would not have been possible without those who have been influential in shaping me. I thank God for giving me a Mom who was my biggest cheerleader in life and who always believed the best. I look forward to worshipping together with her soon. Dad, thank you for your kindness and love. Bobby, thank you for your patience, faithfulness, and strong leadership. Thank you to my twin blessings, Christopher and Joshua. You two have taught me more about life and love than anyone. I'm thankful for all of the years that I had the privilege of homeschooling you and believe that I learned more from you than you did from me. Doris, thank you for taking me in to be able to finish high school in FL. I'm grateful for your loving support. Oma, I thank God for your life. Uncle Lu, thank you for your creative spirit. Thanks to Debra, eternal friend, blessed forever. Thanks to Chris, Brenda, Gabriella, and the prayer supporters and close friends who have encouraged me and prayed for this ministry and work. Most of all, I thank Jesus Christ, who is my magnificent obsession.

Soli Deo Gloria.

About the Cover

In 2013, my mother went home to be with the Lord. On the day that I cleaned out her apartment, I was traveling home with the last of her belongings, grieving and saddened by her loss. As I contemplated her life and death, I looked out of the corner of my eye and saw the beautiful scene while driving by the small pond. After pulling the van over, I walked over and took some photos with my phone. While looking out over the pond, I felt a profound peace at that moment. A peace that gave me the sense that things were going to be okay, and that because of living hope, I would one day see my mom again in heaven.

God reminds us of His creativity and beauty in nature. Beholding a breathtaking scene like a rainbow, a sunset, or colorful garden causes us to step back for a moment and declare that He is a mighty and brilliant artist. He reminds us that He is God and we are not. He is in control of the universe and is so incredibly powerful and big, and we are so, so small. Yet, as small as we are, He has created us, loves us and longs to give us His hope.

We are alive for a reason and a purpose. I pray that you will discover your purpose and what you have been created to do. When you have living hope, you will also experience true love, joy and peace. These treasures make life abundant and full.

Prologue

This journey began in October of 2016. It happened one week after speaking at a women's retreat on the topic of LIVING HOPE, on the first day of our family vacation in the Great Smoky Mountains. It was there that I slowed down and entered into a restful state with God, away from the noise of life. Something special was happening inside of me. I began to write out the books of Ephesians and Colossians, from the Bible, and would stop at various places as led. At those points, I would respond in prayer or in praise, or by putting my thoughts or dreams in an interactive journal. A brand-new burst of poetry and songs began to flow, and continued to flow. When I got home, I began to share some of the poems with individuals, and corporately at church, and other ministry venues as "spoken words." The response was very positive, as people were able to connect with truths about the Lord, and be drawn to Him. Some of the poems have been, and are being, used to help others to be set free, while other poems are bringing others into worship and adoration of the Savior. A song called Deeper, Higher, Wider was also released, which has been sung in churches since September of 2017. God has used, and is using, this newly discovered gift to impart His LIVING HOPE to many. I was never intending to write a book, but it became clear that, as God opened the door to reach out and expand outside of my personal sphere, that I needed to step through and move forward in faith. So, I invite you to embark on a poetic healing journey from brokenness to wholeness, to discover God's heart and His great love for you. May you be brought into a deeper awareness of the Father's love in order to be transformed.

*For the **WORD OF GOD** is alive and active. Sharper than any double-edged sword, it penetrates even to dividing soul and spirit, joints and marrow; it judges the thoughts and attitudes of the heart.*
Hebrews 4:12 (emphasis added)

*...**BE FILLED WITH THE SPIRIT**, speaking to one another with psalms, hymns, and songs from the Spirit. Sing and make music from your heart to the LORD. Always giving thanks to God the Father for everything, in the name of our Lord Jesus Christ.*
Ephesians 5:18c-20 (emphasis added)

Table of Contents

The Journey Begins...

Lord, please draw me close to you.

FIRST LOVE

It's a place of surrender
A place of delight,
Here where I met you,
First love – my delight.

In you alone,
My passionate plea,
Living hope giver,
Purity I see.

Holy fire consume me,
Burn all that must go,
Purify until You are seen,
More than what others know.

Radiant beauty,
Precious Savior,
May my will be thine.
To die and resurrect,
For You a vessel to shine.

BROKEN

Broken I come,
Before your throne,
To lift my burden,
It's yours to own.

My shame and pain
Are taken away.
They're placed in your hands;
It's there they will stay.

Broken, broken before you, my King,
Here at your throne, this song I sing.
Broken, broken before you, my King,
Here at your throne, healing you'll bring.

Guilt and sorrow
Are placed at your feet.
I've let it all go,
In your presence so sweet.

For you are my strength,
Lord, how you love me.
When I look at the cross,
I am finally free.

Broken, broken before you, my King.
Here at your throne, this song I sing.
Broken, broken before you, my King.
Here at your throne, healing you'll bring.

WALKING ON

Situations that are unclear,
Troubled times that are unfair,
I'm letting go… I'm letting go.

It's not certain, can barely see,
The path is rocky, crumbling before me,
Washing away, still I must stay,
And walk on…

Lord, you are here, right beside me,
Showing me the way.
I surrender doubt and worry,
And give to you this day.
I clothe myself with your armor,
To fight this battle, here and now,
With you here, right beside me.

I'm walking on and I don't need to fear,
I'm walking on and I don't need to fear.

HEART

My heart cries out to know You,
Know You more.
My great reward who floods my soul;
Fierce lover, defender, warrior,
My heart is Yours.

It beats with passion,
Holy fire ablaze,
Longing for instruction, refining.
You amaze.

Drinking from Your delights,
Fresh water flows through.
Holy... holy... holy...
I am one with You.

Longing, intense longing,
For Your love's perfect touch.
It heals and restores.
Jesus – I love You so much.

I in You and You in me,
One together,
For all eternity.

SWEET LULLABY

As I crawl into Your lap
And put my head on Your chest,
I listen to Your heart
And feel myself rest.

I listen intently
For Daddy to begin.
He starts His song,
The sound that makes me sing.

Lullaby, sweet lullaby,
The song that makes me smile.
Lullaby, sweet lullaby,
Could we just stay here a while?

Resting here, Your love feels safe,
Your heart I continue to hear.
While trusting and holding You
I say goodbye to fear.

Jesus, Your arms are strong
When mine can't seem to hold.
Resting here, close to You,
Is better than finest gold.

Lullaby, sweet lullaby,
The song that makes me smile.
Lullaby, sweet lullaby,
Could we just stay here a while?

Who Am I?

Lord, please show me who You are and who I am.

PUT OFF – PUT ON

Love is better than hate,
Faith to decide,
To have joy and humility
Rather than pride.

Self-control over anger,
Words that transform,
Thoughts that please God,
Flesh, I won't conform!

Put off the old man, put on the new,
Righteousness, holiness waiting for you.
Put off the old man, put on the new,
Do it for Christ and show the real you.

Meekness, gentleness, truth and respect
Come with the new man... new to expect.
It's better than doubt, impatience and fear;
Spirit of God, You are welcome here!

Put off bad language and sin from your life,
Gossip and slander and words that cause strife.
Put on the new lips, filled with praise from above,
Speaking words of life, healing and love.

Put off the old man, put on the new,
Righteousness, holiness waiting for you.
Put off the old man, put on the new,
Do it for Christ and show the real you.

(based on Colossians 3:8-10)

DO YOU KNOW WHO YOU ARE

When you look at yourself
Whom do you see?
Do you see you
Or do you see Me?

Do you know you're loved deeply,
Cherished, adored?
You are perfect, complete,
And in Christ, one accord.

You're ruling and reigning,
With Him in the heights.
Do you see the warrior
Who conquers and fights?

Do you know that you're royalty,
A child of the King?
Nothing will change that,
No, not anything.

You're accepted, forgiven,
And walking in love.
My beloved you hold
My fiery heart from above.

Your passion and zeal
Is a gift from Me.
My Spirit in you
Is who gives purity.

Walk in the reality
Of who you are,
And My light will shine
Through you like a star.

WE HOPE IN YOU

Lord, we come and we confess
Our love for You has waned.
Ignite us with Your love divine,
Our passion that has drained.

Make her holy, Your bride, we ask,
So that we will be
A radiant church, without stain,
For a blind and lost world to see.

Give us love for You that we once knew
With childlike trust and care,
To be one with You, in love with You,
So the world will be aware.

To be there for each other
In sickness and in pain,
Holding You close to our hearts
For godliness, the greater gain.

May we be one as You were one,
With the Father's plan for You,
A heartbeat of love that shows the world
That we don't just say, but do.

YOU ARE MY EVERYTHING

I love you Lord with all of my heart.
My heart is yours. You are my everything.

I love you Lord with all of my soul.
My soul is yours. You are my everything.

I love you Lord with all of my mind.
My mind is yours. You are my everything.

I love you Lord with all of my strength.
My strength is yours. You are my everything.

My will, my life, all that's in me now,

Belongs to you,
It belongs to you.

You've captured my heart,
Your love that's in me now.
It flows to you.
I'm one with you.

I give up my rights,
And surrender to Your plan.
Now let it flow out to every woman and man.

Your love and truth,
Your glorious truth,
The love that is compelling me to stand.

STAND BACK!

Enemies of God, take heed.
Jesus the victorious has won.
The battle of all ages,
It is finished. It is done.

He has conquered death and sin for all.
No more will you defeat.
You think that you have won,
But His fiery wrath you'll meet.

He put to death guilt and shame.
With a sharp sword He has killed.
Out of His mouth He defeated you.
Faithful and True He has willed.

Sickness, addiction, pain, and strife,
Release your hold right now!
It was nailed to the cross.
By His strong power, you will have to bow.

Love is fierce, love has warred.
Justice has won, blood's been spilled.
The finished work, it was complete,
When the Lamb of God was killed.

He rose victorious, King of all Kings,
With angels by His side.
You must bow to Truth, to the Faithful One,
In me He does reside.

As I speak words of freedom,
Deliverance they will see.
By God's Spirit, the demons take flight,
A hope that sets the captive free.

Victorious one whom I adore,
Hating evil as You do,
Your truth and beauty to behold,
Forever love that is found in You.

REDEMPTION

Worthy are You
Oh heavenly One.
You deserve all glory.
As time unfolds,
The world will hear
Your true redemptive story.

How You bought their hearts
With Your blood.
When You laid it down,
How You raised to life,
Souls from the grave,
To wear righteousness
As a crown.

Worthy are You
Oh glorious One.
Honor belongs to the King.
Praises and worship, all to you Jesus,
Forever we will sing.

Creator of all, You deserve praise
For all that You have done.
For providing, Almighty God,
Redemption through Your Son.

For Your mercy and grace
Praise rings out,
From here to You above.
For your everlasting promises
Show most of all your love!

GRACE

What is this thought of undeserved grace?
A sinner condemned to a tormenting place.
Unable to hope, without a way out,
Weeping and gnashing of teeth all about.

Separated from love and life,
Only surrounded by pain and strife.
Nothing I could do to change my state,
A sinner condemned to a torturous fate.

Until one day Your love reached down.
You said, "You are mine," and gave me a crown.
"Royalty," you said, "You belong to me.
You are mine for all eternity."

Blood was spilled from the cross to the ground.
Dripping with love,
⸱ Each drop made a sound.

Forgiven...
Forgiven...
Forgiven...
Forgiven...

By your sacrifice I can see love,
Healing, right standing with God above.
The arms of the Father have opened wide,
To His kingdom of peace, I've been welcomed inside.
Not by my merit, my works, or my trying,
But on Jesus who hung there, bleeding and dying.

Grace, grace, I belong to the King,
No more condemned, there was nothing to bring.
He did it all, and by faith I'm His heir.
There's new life in Him, I'm now in His care.
Forever I'll be in the place where He lives,
Only by the grace that He lovingly gives.

REMEMBER CHRISTIAN

It's something I must put out of my mind,
When Christians are hateful, mean and unkind.

How they forgot the place where they once stood,
Plucked out of sin's grasp into a land that is good.

It's hard to imagine why some behave as they do,
Lacking love, grace and mercy, just naming a few.

Things a believer should be knowing by now,
When they remember the sacrifice that God did allow.

He chose to take on the darkness and sin,
The perfect Lamb without stain, to invite sinners in.

Yes, some choose to forget all that He said,
Their countenance downcast, looking saddened and dead,

A new way, abundant life, is what He died to bring.
Follow Him and your heart will again begin to sing.

Stop the fighting, holding on to your need to be right.
Petty doctrinal differences, over religion you fight.

When we love deeply, they'll know we're Christians as we say,
The hope and peace that we breathe is the message we display.

Where will the lost, without hope, see the light,
And see Christians love one another, instead of fight?

He died for the pride, the ugliness and pain,
Humble yourself Christian...for the greater gain.

There's a better choice than what the world has to give.
What Jesus did on the cross allows us to live.

The devil wants you in his grasp, so in bondage you'll stay.
Stop the madness, overlook the offense, forgive and turn away.

Lay down your need to judge as you see,
Let love flow through you, no more judge you will be.

Remember, you too were once lost and blind.
Why can't you extend grace and simply be kind?

Your self-righteous behavior is hard to digest,
You carry a spirit of strife and unrest.

Turn to the cross, it's where you'll be free.
You'll remember and be loving as you were created to be.

Don't forget what He did to make you alive.
He laid it all down, so that you would thrive.

Remember the hope that the cross once instilled.
Repent and turn away from your hate, as God has willed.

"Love one another" was His desire for His own.
He stepped close to your ear and whispered with a groan.

With nail-scarred hands and sadness he said,
"Why are you still behaving as though you're still dead?"

RECONCILED

Everything on earth and things hidden above
Was made through Him and for Him
By the Son whom He loves.

In Him, all the fullness of creator God shows,
His supremacy shines wherever He goes.
In Him, things are held together for His sake
To show His power and glory, His glory no one can take.

He deserves the praise, He made it all by His hand.
Things on earth or in heaven,
His word is His command.

This is our life, we won't be shaken,
His gospel of hope, our sins He has taken.

He made us holy so now we can meet,
And talk to our Father and sit at His feet.
By His blood we are His,
With distance away,
As we stand in Christ Jesus,
In Him, complete we will stay.

This is our life, we won't be shaken,
His gospel of hope, our sins He has taken.

It's not by our good works
Or by our efforts that we lend,
But by His blood, reconciled,
Grace He did extend.

This is our life, we won't be shaken,
His gospel of hope, our sins He has taken.
(based on Colossians 1:22)

HE'S IN YOU

His Spirit dwells within,
A temple where there is space.

It used to be empty there.
For Holy Spirit, it's a place
He came to love and fill the void,
That was empty and cold.

New life He birthed, He blew His breath,
And gave eternal springs of gold.

He's in you... He's here today,
He's in you... He's here to stay,
He's in you... I'm here to say,
He's in you!

IT'S WHO YOU ARE

Lord and Master, Reigning King,
Strong and mighty, maker of everything.
You're supremely untainted. You stand apart.
All-knowing of mysteries, You know my heart.

I can't hide from You,
You're present everywhere.
Loving Father, Oh comforter,
I'm always in Your care.

Wise infinite one, You are sovereign,
And You are in control.
You're the healer for brokenness,
Redemption is Your goal.

You're full of good will
Toward the ones You've designed;
Doing what is right, just and fair,
Sanctified by holy fire; refined.

You're faithful to Your promises,
That You don't forget.
You are infinite beyond measure,
At the cross You paid my debt.

You're wrathful and react to evil.
Humanity could not see Your face.
Sin's cost was a sacrifice.
The cross extended grace.

Almighty, all sufficient one,
The great I AM is Your name.
You have supreme authority,
All power, strength and fame.

You spoke all into being,
Creating by Your powerful word.
Perfect, unchanging, immutable One,
Your truths the world has heard.

How Jesus bled and died
And rose victoriously from the grave.
How He did it for LOVE by His undeserved grace,
To heal as well as to save.

Though You're transcendent and exist
Above the universe that we see,
You're personal and intimate,
A loving Father to me.

You're the provider of all good things,
Your perfect love You give.
Your peace passes understanding,
Our sins You do forgive.

To know You more is my reward,
Who You are and about Your ways.
I will worship and praise You
For the rest of all my days.

Going Deeper

Lord, help me to see the reason why I was made.

INTO THE HOLY PLACE

A sacrifice was needed
To cover all our sin,
So that we could go to a place
And boldly enter in.

The blood of goats and bulls
Is needed no more.
Something new provided
A way past sin's door.

Into the Holy place
We can enter, pure.
The blood of the Lamb has cleansed us,
His sacrifice was sure.

He did it all for love's sake,
The perfect sinless one.
For me, for you, for all of us,
Our sins were on the Son.

The great High Priest,
Jesus is His name.
He sacrificed Himself;
He has eternal fame.

All praises to the King,
His glory He will reveal.
All power, strength and majesty,
In His holy presence we kneel.
(based on Hebrews chapter 9)

INCENSE RISING

Released from my heart
An offering is given.
A sacrifice of praise,
From a soul that is forgiven.

The fragrance of incense
Is pleasing to You
When it's praise from a pure heart,
Giving worship that You're due.

Prayers of a righteous child,
They accomplish much.
They're powerful and effective,
With God's heavenly touch.

Wafting up, incense is rising,
The affection sacred and pure.
Opened up by Christ's blood,
The cross became sin's cure.

The sweet smoke of sacrifice,
Fire of God's love divine.
With adoration, a prayer lifted,
May my will be Thine.

Reverence and awe before my God,
A heart that wants to obey.
May it be a sweet aroma
Rising up night and day.

The goods of love are like music's waves,
Rippling out from within.
They're salted, pure and sacred,
Holy fire, without sin.

Love's offering, I give to you.
May its fragrance bring delights
To the only wise and holy Lord,
Smoke rising to the heights.

THE SOUND

There is a sound
Inside of my head;
Loud praise for life,
Something must be said.

Ordained before time, the sound formed.
While in her womb, my ears prepared to hear, "Life! Life!"
"It can be yours – true living, abundant life."
But I couldn't hear a sound, no, for I was dead.
All was silent and dark.
Alone, without hope.

The crashing waves, wind blasting,
Showing something more,
But, unknown to me, void of life.
Until that day, the earth shook and trembled,
The ground split open,
The veil tore down the middle.
The sound, "It is finished." was heard in my ears.
The sound of love in my soul, I began to hear.

Little me heard a sound, the sound of love,
Rippling life into my dry bones.

Love – Love – Love – Love

"I died for you," He said.
One time for all time.
No more death to dread.

I believed the sound of hope.
It breathed into my soul.

Love and truth... He has made me whole.
Now, my heart beats with this love,

The sound
To be heard, hope to be given, life to be spoken.

THE GLORY OF GOD

Shining glory, brightness of His glory,
In His presence are found
Seraphim hovering all around
With their celestial sound.

Two wings to cover their faces,
Two wings to cover their feet.
With two wings they are flying,
His glory do they meet.

Moving around and above His throne,
His majesty they do proclaim.
Holy! Holy! Holy!
Declaring God's greatness and fame.

Calling out to one another
The grand eternal story.
Holy! Holy! Holy!
The whole earth is full of His glory.

The King, seated on the throne,
Worthy, exalted on high.
Heaven's sounds continue on,
Glory to God do they cry.

The temple is filled with the train of his robe
In a place that's filled with smoke.
The doorposts and thresholds trembled and shook
As soon as the angels spoke.

No being could approach the Holy One.
He's set apart, radiant and bright.
Looking out, His blazing eyes
Radiate with love's light.

He wanted us close, not far away,
No more apart, but near,
To come to His throne with confidence,
To approach Him without fear.

We could not meet Him as we were,
Hearts impure and stained with sin.
Into His throne room, we could not go,
Unable to enter in.

Until he gave His only Son, sin's offering to atone,
With love's touch, the stain is gone,
In Him we approach the throne.

We bow before the King most High,
Our heavenly Father we meet.
Cleansed by His blood for all time,
We approach the mercy seat.

Praises and worship unto the King,
With reverence we bow down low.
Giving honor and declaring His worth,
Into His presence we go.
(based on Isaiah Chapter 6:1-8)

PERSECUTED ONE

My heart aches to hear about
Your struggle, anguish and crying.
I pray that you won't give up,
Even when you feel like dying.

I can't imagine the mental challenges
That you face,
Away from your loved ones,
Tortured in a dark, lonely place.

As you suffer for Christ's sake,
You identify with love,
Knowing all that He went through for you,
As innocent as a dove.

With a face radiant
And countenance new
You said, "Father, forgive them,
For they know not what they do."

While you're bleeding and bruised
You won't retaliate.
While opposed and in chains
You don't give in to hate.

While you're abused
There's love on your face.
While you endure beatings
You're aware of His grace.

You consider it a privilege
To suffer for truth's sake.
Christ is exalted in your body,
Your soul they cannot take.

You are not ashamed, dear one.
You give me courage to press on.
I'm more confident because of you,
For on Christ you lean upon.

The chains that you wear,
They are reminders to me
To be bold in the Lord,
More courageous I will be.

Thank you for daring to stand
Even when it's hard to cope.
You've shown through your hardships
That Christ is your living hope.

Persecuted one, there is something
That you need to hear.
Your suffering has prompted me
To proclaim the gospel without fear.

One day, brave one, you will be free
From your bondage and chain.
On you is a crown that reads,
"To live is Christ and to die is gain."

THROUGH THE VEIL

With my face uncovered
I approach the Holy One.
No shame, guilt or condemnation
Are found in the Son.

Fully forgiven by the blood
That Christ shed,
He told me to come,
"With boldness," He said.

My Father is there.
I look for His face.
At the mercy seat,
The most holy place.

Totally accepted
By gracious invitation.
Totally loved
By His proclamation.

Totally forgiven
Is what He decreed,
Part of royal priesthood
Because Jesus did bleed.

He now is my Father,
The glorious King.
With an unveiled face
Let the praises ring!

I'm loved by my Lord.
He has forgiven my sin.
So I could walk forward
And enter right in.

Through the veil,
It's the place for me.
At the feet of my Savior
Is where I long to be.

We don't have to wait
Until our last breath
To spend time at His throne.
It can be now, not only after death.

His presence is here,
His love my reward.
King of my heart,
I know I'm adored.

Radiant beauty,
King of all Kings,
You deserve glory
Over all created things.

Praise to my God,
Lifted high to the One,
Honor and majesty,
To Father, Spirit, Son.

You deserve all
The honor and praise,
Glory to You,
Perfect in all of Your ways.

The song continues
Of life's greatest story,
The Creator of all,
Receiving honor and glory.

THE BODY

The irritation in the oyster
By the rubbing of the sand,
Is like the Body of Christ
Being molded by His hand.

Sometimes it is abrasive
And rubs us the wrong way.
We get hurt and offended
And feel like we don't want to stay.

We say to the foot, "I don't need you"
Or "I don't need you, hand."
"I don't want the irritation;
I want my comfort, understand?!"

The double-edged sword
Is sharp and powerful.
It cuts out the poison.
What it does is wonderful.

Jesus prayed that we would be one
Like He and the Father are,
One purpose and unified,
Without divisions that scar.

We need the Body, in order to grow,
Despite some of the pain that we bear.
We learn to love unconditionally,
For our brothers and sisters, we care.

We each have gifts that we get to use
When we gather as one.
Gifts that encourage and build up
One another in the Son.

How will the world see, if we do not show
The love He wants to display,
To die to ourselves and lay it all down,
"Love one another," Jesus did say.

The Body of Christ, it's part of God's plan
That we will see unfurl,
To make us love more like Him,
On display as a beautiful pearl.

DEEPER LOVE

Who is it that I hear?
Is it my true love walking by?
He calls me His bride,
The apple of His eye.

I hear His footsteps approaching.
I long to see His face.
I wait with anticipation
For us to embrace.

Jesus, sweet Jesus,
You're the King of all that is true.
You're my bridegroom, I'm Your bride.
There's nothing I love more than You.

I delight in Your company
And long to spend time at Your feet,
Sharing thoughts with one another,
For how long are we able to meet?

I like to sit in Your shade,
Content in Your arms my King,
Not a care, concern, or worry,
Just to be here means everything.

Jesus, sweet Jesus,
You're the King of all that is true.
You're my bridegroom, I'm Your bride.
There's nothing I love more than You.

You whisper my name, declare Your love,
Your voice is quiet and clear.
You know my heart, it's tender and soft,
My lover, my bridegroom, my dear.

Your love is strong; it sets me free
To trust you with all that's in me.
My life is yours, together we live
For all eternity.

Jesus, sweet Jesus,
You're the King of all that is true.
You're my bridegroom, I'm Your bride.
There's nothing I love more than You.

TAKE ME TO THE PLACE

Take me to the place
I was born to know.
Into Your heart,
Into Your presence, I go.

Through the veil
To the most Holy place,
Into radiant beauty,
Your presence is the place.

Transformation

Lord, please do Your healing work in me.

FORGIVENESS

A cruel foe that chokes freedom
Is what unforgiveness gives.
Who erects inner walls and prisons,
With grudges, slavery lives!

Unforgiveness chokes life and love.
It keeps us in a bind;
Wearing shackles, willingly,
With thoughts that torment the mind.

There is a way to free ourselves
From this unrelenting hold;
It comes from God, as we release
Our hearts for Him to mold.

When we see what He forgave
In us, our sin-sick soul,
How much we have been forgiven,
Torment stops taking a toll.

So kind and gracious is the LORD
Who forgave us of our sin.
He cleansed us from unrighteousness
For a new way to begin.

Released with smiling freedom,
By His blood we're all set free;
No more a prisoner to that foe
Of unforgiveness, we will be.

No more grudges!
In kindness we let them go.
Knowing that He forgave much,
Forgiveness is what we show.

The undeserved gift that He gave
Unravels all of our "rights."
In victory, the chains are gone;
We're soaring to new heights.

(based on Matthew 18:21-35)

FREEDOM

It is where I want to stay,
Where joy and peace are found.
Like wind on my face,
Hearing freedom's sound.

Freedom, wonderful freedom,
Jesus, in You, I have found.
Freedom, wonderful freedom,
A soul no longer bound.

Warm breeze on a cold day,
It blows its breeze on me.
Where the Spirit of the Lord is,
There is liberty.

Freedom, wonderful freedom,
Jesus, in You, I have found.
Freedom, wonderful freedom,
A soul no longer bound.

No ties on my feet,
I'm smiling and I'm free,
Here to stay forgiven,
Freedom flows out of me.

Freedom, wonderful freedom,
Jesus, in You, I have found.
Freedom, wonderful freedom,
A soul no longer bound.

YOU NEVER CHANGE

Your love is steadfast,
You're always the same.
Your mercy unending,
You're true to Your name.

You're patient and kind
Toward all You have made.
While we were still sinners
Our debts You have paid.

The way some live life
Has nothing to do
With Your loving nature,
Which is faithful and true.

While we were in darkness,
You brought Your great light;
To show us Your beauty,
Your power and might.

There are some that don't show
The love that You gave.
They tend to show hate
In the way they behave.

Your love is irresistible;
No shadow of turning in You.
Your ways are higher than our own,
You don't love the way people do.

God, You are love.
You made us to know You.
Loving others as You show,
You're loving in all you do.

THIS HOPE TO GAIN

One day, in the future,
We will know what it is,
To look into eyes of perfection,
Beauty that is all His.

No more crying or sorrow;
Grief will meet its end.
It, too, will die in its time,
In hearts that He will mend.

Hate and war will be gone;
Deception and lies as well.
Evil and pain, tears and torment
Will be thrown in the pit of hell.

The Christian's hope, a future secure,
Made way by a path of pain,
Christ's blood poured out for sinner's souls,
For all this hope to gain.

A REC TRANSFORMATION

When she walked through the door
I could see it in her eyes;
Pain and hurt compounded,
Heartbreak sounding in her cries.

She sat down and wondered,
"Why am I sitting here?
What's the point of this weekend?
Why did these people come here?"

She felt a sense of doom and dread,
Condemned and guilty for life.
"Why can't I just be killed or die?
It's better than this heart of strife."

She thought that the freedom
Would appear only outside of the wall.
"If I could just get away from this place,
I would be happy and have it all!"

As she began to listen,
She heard a sound begin.
It captured her attention
As love began to win.

Little did she know the One
That she was about to meet,
The author of love she would encounter
As she got up out of her seat.

She knew she was wrong
And was sorry for her sin.
She took a step of faith that day
And let the Savior in.

She believed that He died
On the cross for all evil done.
She reached out and took the hand
Of Jesus Christ, God's Son.

She received His forgiveness
That came down from heaven above.
For the first time in her life
She opened her heart to God's love.

With a new life, she lifted her head.
I could see it in her eyes.
Light, love, joy, and freedom
Were heard within her cries.

She said with a knowing look
Something that she could now see.
She said, "I may be here in this prison,
But I am a woman that is free!"

(written in March 2017, following a transformational ministry time in the WCC Women's Correctional facility at the REC # 72 weekend. The power of the living Christ was experienced by all who were there.
***REC** = Residents Encounter Christ)*

GOODBYE ANXIETY

One night in the dark, in my room,
I felt alone and afraid;
Weary and unable to sleep,
Those tormenting thoughts, they stayed.

I couldn't shake them off. I tried so hard.
They were trying to grab a hold of my soul.
Coming with a cloud of worry,
I felt so out of control.

My body was hot and then it shivered;
Felt my heart pound in my chest.
With tingling arms, I could barely breathe.
Anxiety became my guest.

I was afraid. I thought I was dying.
"No! Don't let that happen to me!"
With sweaty palms, I lifted them up
And cried, "God! Please help! Set me free!"

I cried to the Lord, in my anguish,
"Please intervene," as I lay in this bed.
You've not given me the spirit of fear,
But power, love, and sound mind instead."

"I look to You and place my trust
In Your words of truth for me."
With prayer and petition, I asked the Lord,
"Please make this anxiety flee."

I felt His love, the God of comfort,
The flooding of His peace.
As I kept my trust upon His Word,
The torment began to cease.

In that moment I felt consoled
With a peace that I cannot explain,
A peace that passes all understanding,
My heart was relieved of its pain.

"Thank You for this gift You've given.
You're amazing in all that You do.
Your presence here is all that I need,
And the comfort that is found in You."

Peace, wonderful peace!
I no longer feel afraid.
Anxiety is gone, my soul is calm
From the moment I trusted and prayed.
(based on Philippians 4:6-7)

GOD LAUGHS

"There is no God," the fool said.
God laughs as He displays
Design, patterns, the spectrum of color,
Sameness, variety, chromosomes,
Order - not resulting from chaos -
But by His breath of life.

Worthy of praise, worthy of honor,
Men don't want to acknowledge
Creative works, the miraculous,
Fragrances, glory declared, beauty shines.

Sea creatures, feather of a peacock,
Eye of a whale, vastness of space,
Rivers rushing, thunderings, lightnings,
Flashes of glory, worship, shining all around
By the word of His power.

Warmth of the sun,
Flowers open up their petals,
Unfolding beauty,
New life to behold.

Scurrying creatures, running on the snow,
On trees, they jump from branch to branch,
Dancing the dance of life.

Howling wolves call out,
"I live...my maker...I live!"

Crashing waves, on rocks,
They beat with fury,
Showing unrestrained power.

Tornadoes twisting tumultuously,
Whirling dramatically,
They cease with one word.

The sun's prominences reach out
To grab and consume me,
Pushed back by One who is brighter.

Awesome in splendor and power,
Dazzling beauty all around,
Bearing witness to His greatness, glory, and artistry.

BITTERNESS

A root underground
That one cannot see,
Entangles with others,
Vile network to be.

One spoken word
Causing hurt deep within.
It festers and bleeds,
Producing toxin.

Anger, its friend,
One of the roots,
Smiles gleefully as it
Defiles and pollutes.

Until a moment in time
When the network is seen,
In others affected
By its toxic gangrene.

A spade is thrust in,
Deep under the ground,
To search for the culprit,
Until it is found.

Aha! There it is!
Down deep in the hole,
The hurt that was caused
And the joy that it stole.

My, how you've grown.
You've spread yourself far.
You've entangled yourself
With others to scar.

You vile bitter root,
Your life will now end.
By forgiveness applied,
Forgiveness to rend.

You cannot defile
And spring up anymore.
Your network is broken.
Forgiveness reached to the core.

It broke off your power
To insidiously spread.
Forgiveness released
Has rendered you dead.

Bitter root, you're removed.
You were destined to go.
You couldn't be in the place
Where love needed to grow.

Now that you're completely gone,
I can finally be
Loving and joyful,
Growing peacefully free.
(based on Hebrews 12:15)

DEEPER, HIGHER, WIDER

Your love, oh Lord, is like a well that never ends.
Your kindness and grace, it has no end.

Deeper, higher, wider is Your love;
Way beyond the things that I can see.
Your love, oh Lord, is deeper than the deepest sea.
And, by your love, You set this captive free.

So that's how I can stand here and sing my praise to You,
I am made alive to say, "Jesus I love you."

Your love, oh Lord, is like a well that never ends.
Your kindness and grace, it has no end.

(based on Ephesians 3:16-19)

YOUR HEALING TOUCH

When life first began
There was a heart,
A vacuous place
When we were apart.

It was empty and cold
And deeply alone.
It couldn't feel love,
Was as hard as a stone.

Walls were put up
To block off the sight,
Of love's warm embrace
And love's perfect light.

I tried to be strong
And to love on my own,
But only came up short,
My heart remained as a stone.

Until the day I let You in,
Your love began to soothe
The many hurts over time,
Divine love on the move.

Jesus, Your work at the cross
Poured blood over me,
So I could know love
And truly be free.

Your healing touch,
It reaches in
To heal the brokenness,
To forgive all the sin.

You fix my broken heart.
Deep down in that space.
Your loving touch takes away pain,
Making a holy place.

You've captured my heart.
I'm Yours evermore.
To love as You destined,
With Your love as the core.

FEAR AND CONTROL

"My will, my way,
Is good enough," some may say.
I can do this. See, I've got ability.
I'll plan it out to seek my own serenity.

What I want becomes the aim.
"You stay there, I'll stay here,
As we play out this game."

Love disengaged,
Fear and control
Hold their squeezing grip
Upon the captive's soul.

Sucking out light's pure shine,
"We'll kill you," they say.
Torment holds with choking grasp
When the beloved tries to pray.

The King of Glory pursues
The one He came to save,
And rescues with His loving hand,
Blood dripping, in love, He gave.

Come closer to me.
It's okay, I'm here to heal.
Trust me with your heart;
I know how you feel.

I love you precious one.
You're my delight.
You can trust me with everything.
I'll do what is right.

Take my hand and never look back.
Walk forward in this new way,
Trusting me with new found freedom
As you rise to begin each day.

THE TONGUE

Like a rudder that steers a ship,
It is extremely small,
Turns the course of the mightiest vessel,
Making the secure man fall.

Like a spark, it's small but potent;
It can cause a raging flame.
Forests burned down by one little spark,
Destruction is its name.

It's a world of evil in a man.
It corrupts and plans to cause death.
With a stubborn will, it kicks and drags,
Choking out all of life's breath.

No human being can tame it;
It cannot be controlled.
With an unsurrendered heart,
It's impossible to hold.

If allowed to continue,
It will eventually win.
The tongue of death will achieve its goal
Of killing others by its sin.

Truths of God's Word, they transform
The hardest of heart.
The Spirit of God does His work
To heal the inner part.

He breathes His breath of life;
Wisdom He does provide.
He creates and forms a new heart
So the love of God will preside.

When a heart is changed by Christ,
Becoming soft, tender, and feeling,
Truths are received and start to work,
Releasing life, love, and healing.

The tongue of the wise brings life.
It spreads its words to all.
Out of the heart, the mouth speaks
For others to hear life's call.

Healing, love, joy, and peace
Are found in the heart within:
A contrite soul who prays to God,
"Lord, keep my tongue from sin."

The tongue is a powerful force,
Causes death and ripping apart.
It can also produce vibrant life
When it speaks from a transformed heart.

(based on James 3: 1-12)

BREAKING FREE

Soaring bird, you flap your wings,
Because you want to fly.
Outside of your cage, you want to go,
To rise high into the sky.

The door has been opened.
Why won't you fly out?
You bang against the wall of the cage.
You thrash yourself about.

Can't you see your path to be free,
Exactly what you have wanted to do?
To fly, to soar, out of your space,
To live your life anew.

Go to the door, the way, the truth,
And you will be made free
To be the bird that glides with power,
As you were created to be.

At the door, you stretch your chest.
Lose the fear you're not to keep.
With some faith, you prepare
To take the initial leap.

Up into the room you go,
Flying high and wide.
As the door is opened,
You continue to the outside.

Fresh air, bright sun, warm breeze,
Are things outside of the door.
You spread your wings and take to flight,
Into the sky you soar.

Joyful bird, you swerve and turn,
As the wind carries you along.
There's no more that you need to do,
Than to trust in freedom's song.

The melody of freedom will carry you far,
To where you want to go -
To make your dreams reality,
As you glide within the wind's flow.

Living Out New Life

Lord, would you please use me to touch others?

IDENTITY

Young people, because I love you,
I have something to say
To you about God's love,
His truth and His way.

The lies you've believed
About yourself, they're not true.
They're wrapped with a bow
And given to you.

The world gives its messages.
To you, they have lied.
They have nothing to do
With the person inside.

Falsehoods that shape,
What you believe about you,
Tell you identity
Is based on what you do.

When your friends, fashion,
Appearance, and "likes"
Are where you find significance,
False identity strikes!

Money and accomplishment
Does not make the real you.
They are only outward things
That show others what you do.

Who you are does not come from you.
It comes as a gift from God.
He sent His Son to die on the cross
To rescue all who were flawed.

When trust is placed upon the Son,
And faith applied as well,
Your identity becomes His,
Right down to the smallest cell.

Your life is in Him now.
That lost young person has died.
You're now a new creature in Christ.
You have a new identity inside.

You belong to Him.
You're cherished, beloved, adored.
You are more than a conqueror,
By a gracious and loving Lord.

He says, "You are mine.
You belong to me.
You're part of my family now,
A masterpiece of royalty."

You're blessed. Do you realize the gift
That has been given to you?
It changes everything.
You have an identity that's new!

There's nothing you did to earn it.
It did not come from you.
It came from the Master Craftsman,
Whose name is Faithful and True.

You are worth fighting for.
Precious one, I can help you to see
That He laid His life down for you
To be the person you were destined to be.

You're righteous, clean, and without stain.
He took away every ounce of shame.
Time to walk in your brand-new life,
To carry the torch of love's flame.

It's not what you feel
That dictates who you are.
It's who HE DECLARES YOU TO BE -
You are His shining star.

As you lay down your will
For the one who laid it down for you,
Genuine purity, kindness, and love
Will show in what you do.

There is no greater honor
Than to live your life for God:
To praise Him with all that's in you,
His greatness to applaud.

In a moment, this life will end
And you will see Him on His throne.
From your memory, He will remove
Those lies you tried to own.

The real you will be revealed
In this life or on that day.
Believe the truth about yourself
And live it out today!

WALK IN LOVE

What does it mean to walk in love
The way God designed?
Is it simply a shifting
Of ways we think with our mind?

To consider others and put them first,
So they are priority one;
To lay down our lives for another,
To exemplify the Son.

Their needs before mine.
They are more important than me.
Preferring what they want
With a love that they can see.

They will know that they're loved.
They will see it and will feel it.
It comes from the heart,
From the core of the spirit.

My heart has been changed.
I'm no longer the same.
Jesus is my passion.
I'm made to walk as a loving flame.

To deliberately show love,
Wherever I go,
Spilling out everywhere,
So the Savior they will know.

He's attractive and beautiful.
He lives inside of me.
His Spirit draws others in,
So His love they, too, can see.

How does one truly walk in love
While on planet earth?
It's by realizing that we're IN HIM
At the moment we received new birth.

It's not your love anymore.
It doesn't come from you.
God's love unconditional;
It's what has made you new.

There are ways to love
In thoughts or in deed.
One thing that I know for sure,
His love is what we need.

INTO THE WATERS

One church, one body,
Diverse, yet together in love;
Denominational barriers broken
By Father, Son, and Spirit above.

testing the waters

In the Trinity, there is unity,
Oneness in purpose and plan.
Jesus prayed that we would be one
As He and the Father began.

stepping into the waters

Many churches, from all around,
Together in prayer, hearts are knit.
Seeking Him in one accord,
To Jesus our hearts we commit.

wading in the waters

We are one in the bond of love;
Can't tell the difference among all.
As the power of God is released,
We embrace God's unity call.

ready to jump

Together we are growing closer,
As one body, hand in hand.
Hope for the world from God's view,
For the glory of Jesus, we stand.

jumping into the waters

Together, working for Jesus,
Impacting the region for good,
Spreading the good news all around,
Loving one another as we should.

swimming in the waters

Completely submerged in the river,
His love flooding us deep within,
Touching the city of Hartford,
Seeing His glory and watching love win.

*(written for **The Hartford Project** in June 2017 as a declaration of unity)*

CORNERSTONE

Battering rain, howling wind,
Roaring rumble, lightning flash
On the house upon the sand.
It toppled down with a crash.

A message they were destined to hear;
For strangers, a truth to behold.
"I don't believe it," some people said.
"I'm content wearing my blindfold."

The stone that the builders rejected
Was a stumbling block.
It was tested and was tried,
The one foundational rock.

Prophecies spoke of the stone,
The One that would make them secure.
It would ensure stability,
The construction solid and sure.

The principal stone,
That joins Gentile and Jew,
Within God's Holy household.
Those who find it, they are few.

Unifying Cornerstone,
Jesus is His name.
The one who truly believes in Him
Will never be put to shame.

In Him, we're family;
We're not strangers anymore.
We are welcomed in.
It's what He gave His life for.

The members of His household
Are temples where He lives.
He's the sure foundation.
Eternal life He gives.

Jesus, You're the stone.
On You, my house stands tall.
The winds will beat against it
But it will never fall.

Jesus, Rock of Ages,
Marvelous to be known,
Salvation is found in no one else.
You're the precious Cornerstone.
(based on Ephesians 2:19-21)

UNION

Apart, a soul divided,
Away from Him too long.
With a downcast countenance,
The bride desperately sings her song.

Where is my beloved?
I can't find Him in the dark!
Turbulent chaos and confusion,
All is desolate and stark.

Where is my beloved?
I can't find Him near to me!
I'm lost! Where can I find Him?
There's just blackness that I see.

The passion of the bridegroom
Longing for His bride,
His heart of anticipation
Welling up inside.

His treasured possession
Coming on bended knee,
Forsaking all other gods,
To dwell in the place of safety.

I'm turning away from false ideas,
Leaving them all behind.
Delivered from the cold untruths
That kept me dead and blind.

My heart is awakened
By a voice so tender and clear.
With desperation I cry out,
Oh my Jesus! Be ever near!

Hungering to be close,
One spirit, one purpose in You,
Knowing that this is the closest place
Of intimate love I once knew.

It's the dwelling place of perfect peace,
Pure love, present and strong,
Perfect light, Christ in me,
In You where I belong.

It's my eternal home,
Abiding in the vine,
Delighting in Your many pleasures,
Your radiance to shine.

Flowing love forever,
To know Your gentle heart,
Never wanting to stray away,
To times when we're apart.

Oh, to know You more,
Faithful lover of my soul,
The union together that we share,
Your heart becomes my goal.

To love as You love,
Your heart flowing out of me,
To be about my Father's business,
Shining Your radiant beauty.

POUR OUT

As You have poured in,
Lord, may we pour out
To all those around us,
From lovers devout.

You have given much,
The treasure that we hold.
We can't keep it to ourselves,
The message we were told.

The gospel, Your story,
Extravagant gift.
For those dead in sin
and destruction; You lift.

The desire that's Yours,
Knowing Your heart:
Sharing love, spilling out,
Working, doing our part.

We weep as You do,
For the souls that are dead.
You're burdened for them,
So Your Word must be spread.

You have given freely
Your eternal love to us.
Send us out, to pour out,
Your truths that we discuss.

It's not our message
For the world to be told.
It's your love and your truth.
Your Spirit makes us bold.

We're living Hope-givers
Of the truths we've believed.
It's not just for us to have,
But for others to receive.

Freely flowing like a stream;
Not stagnant, but alive.
As we give our lives to You,
You cause us all to thrive.

How can we stay silent
When we hear cries for release?
No way out from the fire
Where screams will never cease!

Can we hear the groans and wailing,
Those cries that never die?
We must rescue more souls
Because time is flying by!

If we don't, then who will?
The ministers we pay?
No! You told *us* to go
And gave us the words to say.

Now is the time to share Your love,
Your gospel to the lost.
Fully surrendered, fully yours,
Our lives become the cost.

Desire for the nations,
You pour out to them in love
By sending people filled with You,
With wisdom from above.

You love the world so much,
That to the world You gave
Your only Son to die for them;
He gave His life to save.

May we fulfill Your purposes
And Your redemptive plan,
To take this message to the world,
To every woman and man.

To act justly, love mercy,
And walk humbly in Your name,
May this gospel be poured out
For Jesus' glory and fame.

CLOSING PRAYER

May you, the reader of this work, be blessed and have a deeper awareness of the Father's love. May your faith be ignited by the Spirit's power so that you may be drawn into deeper intimacy with the Lord Jesus Christ. As you ask, seek, and knock, may He fulfil your deepest desire to know Him more as you surrender all to His Lordship. May God reveal the many facets of His love for you so that you would truly know Him and make Him known.
~Elicia

Praise be to the God and Father of our Lord Jesus Christ! In his great mercy he has given us new birth into a living hope through the resurrection of Jesus Christ from the dead, and into an inheritance that can never perish, spoil or fade. This inheritance is kept in heaven for you, who through faith are shielded by God's power until the coming of the salvation that is ready to be revealed in the last time.
I Peter 1:3-5

For I am not ashamed of the gospel, because it is the power of God that brings salvation to everyone who believes: first to the Jew, then to the Gentile.
Romans 1:16

Made in the USA
Middletown, DE
10 December 2020